Love In A Tweet

Rian Malan

Cover design by: Bianca Vosloo

Epigraph

I love those who love me,
and those who seek me find me.
With me are riches and honor,
enduring wealth and prosperity.

- Proverbs 8:17-18

Love!
Love God above everything! Show it with unwavering obedience.
Love!
Love others as yourself! Show it by living a holy and righteous life.

- Love In A Tweet

Contents

Acknowledgements

Soli Deo Gloria.

"Everything comes from God." Thank you, Lord, for the guidance and the strength to persevere. If this work can make a humble contribution to help even only one person to grasp Your love, it would have served its purpose.

To the greatest worldly gifts God gave me, my wife of noble character and my kids and grandkids, I express my sincere love for the love you have shown in words and in works over more than 50 years. May God love you and bless you for that.

Rudolf Markgraaff, God compels me to once again thank you for listening to Him and inviting me to that divine intervention at Wedderville in 2021. Both "Blessing In A Tweet" and now "Love In A Tweet" emerged as a result of the moment the three of us had that day.

Alyson Rockhold, your invaluable craftsmanship in helping with the writing of the Tweets not only showcased the great gifts God bestowed on you but also threw the spotlight on your deep love for God. Never stop using your gifts to glorify God. Thank you.

Without BibleGateway, the asking, seeking, and knocking for insight into the love and will of God would have been quite an arduous task.

Preface

I've believed in God my whole life. But as everything fell apart in 2021, I leaned on Him in a whole new way. When Covid took my job and my stability, I turned to the Bible for comfort and help.

Devouring the 727,969 words of scripture in 3 months was like eating through the entire menu of the finest restaurant in the world. I tasted and saw that the Lord is good, and I couldn't keep that goodness to myself.

So, I asked God what He wanted me to do with what He'd taught me. That's when *Blessing In A Tweet* came to me. The mission of *Blessing In A Tweet* was to compile a tweet of precisely 140 characters that would serve as a daily reminder of how God calls me to live my life.

> **Love, trust and obey God and His Way.**
> **Do to others as you want others to do to you.**
> **Pray and hope through Jesus with faith and thanksgiving.**
> *- Blessing In A Tweet*

The first word of the *Blessing In A Tweet* is "love." Its placement is intentional. The Bible includes a lot of teachings on love. In fact, "love" is listed 551 times in the Bible (NIV).

So, *Love In A Tweet* is a natural progression from *Blessing In A Tweet*. Whereas my first book condensed the whole Bible into a tweet, this book distills the Bible's teachings on love into 140 characters.

When I started writing this book, I was consumed with praying and reading about love. Every day I would ask the Holy Spirit for insights about love. *Love In A Tweet* is the fruit of that labor.

As I studied the Bible's teachings on love, one question kept plaguing me: Am I living a life of love? Perhaps this question haunts you, too. I'll share God's answer in the following pages.

May the gracious Lord open your eyes, ears, and heart as you read *Love In A Tweet*. May it deepen your love for God, yourself, and your neighbor. May you live a life of love.

Rian Malan

Introduction

There are Bible verses that scare me. Descriptions of the end times and the gory details of Old Testament wars would give anyone nightmares. But, I believe the most unsettling verse in the Bible is John 21:16.

In this passage, Jesus appears to the disciples after rising from the dead. He provides a miraculous catch of fish, and they eat breakfast together. Then comes the line that makes me tremble. Jesus turns to Peter and says, "Simon son of John, do you love me?"

Jesus asks Peter this question three times. And each time that Peter says "Yes," Jesus replies with a command to feed His lambs or take care of His sheep. It almost sounds like Jesus is saying, "Prove it!" The Bible records that Peter is hurt by this interrogation. Imagine how terrible it would feel to sacrifice everything to follow Jesus and then have Him question your love.

It's scary to think about Jesus asking me the same thing: Rian Malan, do you love me? Of course, I love You, my Lord! But does my life show it? Am I displaying that love in tangible and real ways? Am I feeding his lambs and caring for his sheep? Am I living a life of love?

I want to love God the way He desires to be loved. I want to love God with my whole heart, mind, soul, and strength. This is not transactional love. I am not trying to earn my salvation. Instead, living a life of love is a way of obeying, honoring, and serving the God who first loved me and still loves me.

This book is for people who have already acknowledged Jesus Christ as the Son of God, believe that He was raised from the dead, and, by doing that, received the free gift of salvation. It's for believers who want their love for God to overflow into all of their thoughts, words, and deeds. And it's also for skeptics who feel attracted to the love of Christ but repelled by unloving Christians.

If that's you, then this book will provide you with three assurances:

1) Wisdom, understanding, and insight into how God views love
2) Practical guidelines for loving as God calls us to love
3) Affirmation that you are living a life of love

This book is built on the Bible's firm foundation. We will return to the scriptures for wisdom again and again throughout the following pages. And I trust that the same Holy Spirit who guided me to write these words will also open the eyes of your heart to know God more and more as we journey together.

My prayer is that by the end of this book, you will be able to confidently answer Jesus' question with "Yes, Lord, I love you!" And then you will hear God say, "Well done, good and faithful servant. I have prepared inconceivable blessings for you."

CHAPTER 1

It's all about God

Whoever does not love does not know God, because God is love.
- 1 John 4:8

"God is love" is one of the most important statements in the Bible (1 John 4:8). Yet, it is often overlooked. Instead, people act like "God just cares about rules," "God is hateful," or even "God is irrelevant."

Yet, the Bible tells us that "God is love." And that has profound implications for what it means to follow God.

God

Before we delve into God's love and what that means for our lives, we must start with God Himself. For without faith in God, the rest of this book will be meaningless.

God is "the Alpha and the Omega, the First and the Last, the Beginning and the End" (Revelation 22:13). God has always been, is now, and always will be.[1] God is all-powerful and all-knowing. He is our Sovereign King.

God is described in so many ways throughout the scriptures. (You can read about many of them in Annexure A). However, it is important to note that no matter how much we learn about God, understanding Him will always be beyond us. As Romans 11:33 says,

> *"Oh, the depth of the riches of the wisdom and knowledge of God!*
> *How unsearchable his judgments,*
> *and his paths beyond tracing out!"*

God created human beings in His likeness, and our lives are in His hands.[2] We are here to fulfill God's purpose and not our purpose. God's purpose for us is to glorify Him. [3]

God's love led Him to...

> Create us
> Give us the free will that caused us to turn away from Him
> Make a Grand Plan to save us

God's Grand Plan started with Jesus' death and resurrection. That is how God opened the door for us to enter His Kingdom and have eternal life.[4] But the plan doesn't end there.

God's ultimate goal is for His dwelling place to be among His people. As scripture says, "They will be his people, and God himself will be with them and be their God. He will wipe every tear from their eyes. There will be no more death or mourning or crying or pain" (Revelation 21:3-4). God will achieve that through the Second Coming of Jesus Christ.

The grand prize of faith in Jesus and living a life of love is eternal life in heaven. Yet, God also makes us this wonderful promise: "Give and you will receive. Your gift will return to you in full - pressed down, shaken together to make room for more, running over" (Luke 6:38). So, if we live a life of love, it will also return in overflowing measures for all the days of our lives.[5]

We are in the waiting time between Jesus' first and second coming. Yet, we are not called to wait passively. We don't want to be like the five foolish virgins who didn't have enough oil in their lamps when the bridegroom arrived (see Matthew 25:1-13). In the waiting time, we are called to love. Love In A Tweet was written as a guide for this time of waiting.

God's Love

In Christ, we see that God's love is an incredible, sacrificial, all-encompassing love. For God's love led Him to sacrifice His only Son to give us eternal life. [6] And truly "greater love has no one than this: to lay down one's life for one's friends" (John 15:13).

God moves towards His people in love, pursuing their hearts and drawing them into the abundant life He's prepared for them. Through Christ, God offers us eternal life and welcomes us into His Kingdom of righteousness, peace, and joy.[7]

God invites all people into His Kingdom, but it's up to us to RSVP to His invitation. We can do that by declaring with our mouths that Jesus is Lord and believing in our hearts that God raised Him from the dead.[8] It's as easy as that - a gift from our loving Father, free of charge.

Once we accept God's gift of salvation, He sends us the Holy Spirit to guide us in the ways of love. God wants us to learn to rely on the Spirit's inner promptings so that we can share God's love with the world. Then our lives will be like rays of light shining goodness, righteousness, and truth into the dark world.[9]

Therefore, God's love is displayed in Christ Jesus and through the gift of eternal life. God's love lives in us through the Holy Spirit. And God's love is revealed to us through the scriptures.

Our Response to God's Love

When someone gives you a gift, it's polite to write a thank you letter. The bigger the gift, the more we feel compelled to thank the giver. If someone gave you a small gift like a pair of socks, you might give a simple thank you note out of a feeling of obligation. But if someone gave you a huge gift like a new car, you would probably be overflowing with gratitude and searching for a way to properly express it. One measly card wouldn't be nearly enough! You would want to thank the giver every time you saw them. So, how can we thank God for the inconceivably amazing gift of salvation and eternal life? The Bible tells us that "this is love for God: to keep his commands" (1 John 5:3). The word 'keep' is a verb, it requires action. God's love compels us to take action. Jesus tells us that the greatest action we can take is to love the Lord our God with all our heart, and with all our soul, and with all our mind, and with all our strength. And the second greatest commandment is to love our neighbor as ourselves.[10]

Therefore, God is love and the greatest of God's commands are to love God and love others. That is what *Love In A Tweet* is all about.

Action Items:
1) Prayerfully read through the list of God's characteristics in Annexure A. Praise God for who He is!
2) Many Christians fall into the trap of spending most of their prayer time just asking for things. They forget to praise God! If you've fallen into that trap, confess it now and ask for forgiveness.
3) Ask God how He wants you to grow a habit of praise. If it's helpful, return to the list in Annexure A regularly in order to prompt you to praise God more and more.

CHAPTER 2

The Tweet

Love In A Tweet condenses the Bible's teaching on love into the 140 characters of a tweet.

Just as you memorize Bible verses and inspirational quotes, I hope you will commit these 4 simple lines to memory. Then they will be ready to help when you question what God is calling you to do. My hope is that this tweet will become a filter through which you make your decisions and determine your courses of action.

Don't let its simplicity distract you from its depth of wisdom and truth. In the next 3 sections, we'll go through the main parts of the tweet, explain its biblical basis, and help you apply it to your life.

The Greatest Commandments

Love In A Tweet encapsulates the two greatest commandments and, therefore, God's guidance for how to live.

In Matthew 22:34-40, we read that the Pharisees got together to try to trick Jesus by asking the hardest question they could imagine: "Which is the greatest commandment in the Law?" Now, to fully grasp how difficult this question was, you have to realize that there are 613 laws in the Old Testament.

The Pharisees thought they had given Jesus a challenge to choose one law from so many options, but Jesus easily answered, "Love the Lord your God with all your heart and with all your soul and with all your mind." Jesus identified this as the first and greatest commandment.

Then He goes above and beyond what the Pharisees asked by also identifying the second greatest commandment: "Love your neighbor as yourself."
So, you can see that the structure of the Tweet follows the structure of Jesus' answer:

Jesus says	The Tweet echoes
Love the Lord your God with all your heart, soul, and mind	Love God above everything!
Love your neighbor as yourself	Love others as yourself!

Our mission, therefore, is to love and to love!

What is love?

So, let's go back to the basics and define love. First, it's important to realize that love is both a noun and a verb. According to the Merriam-Webster Dictionary, love in noun form means "a strong feeling of liking and caring for another arising out of kinship or personal ties." As a verb, love means "to hold dear."

Love is both affection (noun) and action (verb). This really hit home to me when I was writing my last book, *Blessing In A Tweet*. I was reading a lot of Bible verses about love and began to notice a pattern in my own life. My wife and daughter would greet me every morning with, "I love you!" However, I rarely returned the sentiment.

It wasn't because I don't love my wife and daughter. In fact, it's just the opposite. I love them so much that I want to show them my love instead of just talking about it. To be honest, I used to think that saying, "I love you," was quite meaningless. I didn't want to say it, I wanted to show it!

As I was writing this book, I realized that both are important: affection and action, words and deeds, nouns and verbs. But what does that look like in everyday life?

We cannot discuss love without reading 1 Corinthians 13. This chapter has been copied in its entirety for easy reference - see Annexure C and make a point of reading it before you continue here.

This well-known and often quoted chapter was written by God through the Apostle Paul. Paul breaks the chapter up into three sections:

1. Love's great importance
2. Defining love
3. The immortality of love

Love's great importance

The chapter starts with Paul listing out some of the most spectacular feats of faith: speaking in tongues, prophesying, moving mountains, giving everything to the poor, and sacrificing yourself for God. Then he says that these amazing accomplishments are worthless if they are not done with love.

Defining love

Love is patient, kind, and rejoices with the truth.
Love does not envy, boast, dishonor others, keep records of wrongs, or delight in evil.
Love is not proud, self-seeking, or easily angered.
Love always protects, trusts, hopes, and perseveres.

The immortality of love

"And now these three remain: faith, hope and love. But the greatest of these is love" (I Corinthians 13:13).

Imagine the day when you enter heaven. Your faith is complete because you see God face to face. And there is nothing left to hope for because you have more than you could have ever wanted. Faith and hope are no longer needed in God's glorious kingdom.

You have entered a realm where love is the way of life. A realm where the God of love abides. You will be surrounded by love, filled with love, and overflowing with love.

How do I love God?

Carefully read and meditate on the following:

"But if anyone obeys his word, love for God is truly made complete in them"
(1 John 2:5).

"In fact, this is love for God: To keep his commands"
(1 John 5:3).

It's pretty clear that love for God involves keeping His commands. So we must be regularly in God's word, studying and learning His commands so that we can follow them. We must bind them on our fingers and write them on the tablet of our heart.[1] This is love in action, a way of honouring our Holy God and expressing our deep gratitude for all of the gifts He's given us.

We will go into more detail about how we can show our love for God in the next chapter. This will involve digging into scripture as well as providing practical applications for loving God in our daily lives.

How do I love others?

Jesus provides more insight on this in Matthew 7:12, "So in everything, do to others what you would have them do to you, for this sums up the Law and the Prophets."

It is very clear: Love others as you love yourself by doing to them what you wish they'd do to you.

Have you ever said something and immediately saw a look of pain on the other person's face? Imagine if you could've stopped before speaking and asked yourself, "Would I like someone to say this to me?" Most likely, you wouldn't have moved forward with that hurtful statement if you had asked that question first.

Now, of course, there are gray areas in life where you're not quite sure what the right thing is to think, feel, say, or do. It isn't always so clear-cut. Thankfully, God gives us more guidance.

Every Christian has been given the Holy Spirit to help them discern between right and wrong. Wisdom is available to us, we just have to ask. As James 1:5-6 says:

"If any of you lacks wisdom, you should ask God, who gives generously to all without finding fault, and it will be given to you. But when you ask, you must believe and not doubt, because the one who doubts is like a wave of the sea, blown and tossed by the wind."

God has also given us the wisdom of scripture to guide our actions. The Bible provides a guide to living a holy and righteous life like Jesus did. That is why reading scripture is an essential part of a Christian's life.

Therefore, we love others by treating them as we want to be treated. And, in moments of uncertainty, we ask the Holy Spirit to help us speak and act in loving ways.

And so I join with Paul and pray this over you as you continue discovering the power and miracle of God's love:

"This is my prayer: that your love may abound more and more in knowledge and depth of insight, so that you may be able to discern what is best and may be pure and blameless for the day of Christ, filled with the fruit of righteousness that comes through Jesus Christ - to the glory and praise of God"
(Philippians 1:9-11).

Action Items:

1)   Set a timer for 10 minutes. Read through 1 Corinthians 13 (found in Annexure C) slowly, savoring the beautiful description of love. Ask God to guide your thoughts as you read through the passage a few times. If a word or phrase catches your attention, sit with it and ask God what He wants to teach you about love.

2)   Is there a time in the past week when you've acted unlovingly to God, yourself, or others? Confess that to God now. Then ask God for help to act more lovingly in the future.

CHAPTER 3

Love God

Love!
Love God above everything! Show it with unwavering obedience.
Love!
Love others as yourself! Show it by living a holy and righteous life.
-Love In A Tweet

These are the key Bible verses for this section:

"I am the Lord your God...showing love to a thousand generations of those who love me and keep my commandments."
- Exodus 20:2,6

"Love the Lord your God with all your heart and with all your soul and with all your mind and with all your strength."
- Mark 12:30

This chapter focuses on the first half of Love In A Tweet, which is broken into three main topics:

1) Love God
2) Love God above everything
3) Show it with unwavering obedience

Love God

The notion of loving God should not be difficult to grasp:

He is our Creator and Sustainer.

He's given us all of creation including the plants, animals, and minerals that we need to survive.

Everything belongs to Him, and He holds our lives in His hands.[1]

Instead of leaving us in our sinful, fallen state and condemning us to death, God sacrificed his one and only son, Jesus Christ, to save us.

When we accept this gift from the cross, God makes a covenant with us.[2]

> He forgives our sins.
> He gives us eternal life.
> He puts His law in our minds and writes it on our hearts.[3]

When we think about everything that God has done for us, it is easy to shout "I love you, Lord!" But our love for God must go beyond mere lip service.

How are we called to love God?

First, we must love God completely. This means that we love Him with all we have. [4] We love Him more than we love anybody else.[5] And we worship Him as the one and only God.[6]

Second, we need to put our love into action. This starts with obeying God's laws. [7] Then it continues with following in Jesus' footsteps and trying to live a holy and blameless life.[8] In this way, we follow the scriptural command to imitate God by walking in love.[9]

If we love God with our whole being and put that love into action, then our lives will begin to bear fruit. And John 15:8 tells us, "By this My Father is glorified, that you bear much fruit."

What's the bottom line?

No love for God, no eternal life. No love for God, no forgiveness of sins. No love for God, no righteousness, joy, or peace.

Love God above everything!

We live in a loud, busy world that is full of distractions. It is easy to fill our schedules with tasks, our minds with ideas, and our hearts with competing affections.

Yet, Jesus was very clear about where our priorities should be: "Love the Lord your God with **all** your heart and with **all** your soul and with **all** your mind and with **all** your strength" (Mark 12:30, emphasis added).

Loving God comes first and then everything else we do should flow out of that love.

I'm reminded of a recent conversation with my young granddaughter, Zoe.

On my way to drop her off at school, I asked her, "Who do you love most?"

Her answer was quick and without hesitation, "My mom!"

Oh, if only we could all have the kind of dedication and deep love for God that Zoe has for her mom. She loves her simply and completely. There are no competing interests or alternate answers. That is the kind of love we should have for God.

Of course, being a grandfather who is literally writing a book about loving God, I took the opportunity to teach Zoe about loving God above everything, even her mom. I pray God will grow that seed of faith in her life.

While it is understandable for a young child to lack the spiritual maturity to love God above everything, we are held to a higher standard. We must love God more than we love our spouse, our children, or ourselves.

This can be challenging. Think of the story of Abraham being asked to sacrifice his only son, Isaac. God needed to know that Abraham loved God more than he loved his son (see Genesis 22:1-18).

And then there is Jesus' saying that "Anyone who loves their father or mother more than me is not worthy of me; anyone who loves their son or daughter more than me is not worthy of me" (Matthew 10:37). We are truly called to love God more than anyone or anything else.

We should love God above everything because He is the Alpha and the Omega, the Beginning and the End. All love comes from Him and our love begins with Him, in Him, and for Him.[10]

Let us also never forget that God is a jealous God.[11] We cannot allow competing interests to tear us away from our love for God. We are called to love Him with our ALL!

Show it with unwavering obedience.

Love starts with an emotion or a feeling. I vividly remember when I saw my wife for the first time at a school party over fifty years ago. I was immediately attracted to and interested in her. But I did not say, "I love her!" Neither did I say, "I will do anything for her."

Instead, all that I knew was that I had an indescribable and intense feeling of affection for her.

The more that I got to know her, that initial emotion blossomed into true love.

And that love was on display in how I spoke to and interacted with her. It wasn't enough for me to say, "I love you!" I had to show it in how I treated her and cared for her.

The same is true for how we love God. Love starts as affection and grows into action. This notion is on display throughout scripture. Here are two examples from Jesus' teachings:

"Not everyone who says to me, 'Lord, Lord,' will enter the kingdom of heaven, but only the one who does the will of my Father who is in heaven" (Matthew 7:21).

Why do you call me, 'Lord, Lord,' and do not do what I say?" (Luke 6:46)

It doesn't matter that we affectionately call Jesus our Lord if we aren't doing something with that love. Look at the above verses again. Notice the words "does" and "do." Jesus is reminding us that our affection should be shown in our actions.

1 John 5:3 says: "For this is the love of God, that we keep his commandments. And his commandments are not burdensome." So, in the next section, we will review what we're called to do by looking at God's commandments.

It can be overwhelming to search through scriptures and find so many rules and laws and lists of dos and don'ts. So, we will simplify it by looking at the main laws in the Old Testament, the new covenant in the New Testament, and the life of the Spirit.

Main Laws of the Old Testament

We've already covered the two greatest commandments:
-       Love the Lord your God with all your heart and with all your soul and with all your mind (Deuteronomy 6:4-5).
-       Love your neighbor as yourself (Leviticus 19:18).

And most of us know the Ten Commandments found in Exodus 20:1-17:
1)   You shall have no other gods before me.
2)   You shall not worship idols.
3)   You shall not misuse the name of the Lord your God.
4)   Remember the Sabbath day by keeping it holy.
5)   Honor your father and your mother.
6)   You shall not murder.
7)   You shall not commit adultery.
8)   You shall not steal.
9)   You shall not lie.
10)   You shall not covet.

All Christians are called to keep these commandments with unwavering obedience. Our love of God should compel us to follow them. Living out these commands is how our affection turns into action.

However, you'll notice that each of these commands is originally from the Old Testament. The Old Testament is based on the old covenant between God and His people. Jesus said that He did not come to abolish the Law of the Old Testament, but to fulfill it.[12] We read about Jesus' fulfillment of the law in the New Testament, which also comes with a new covenant and new commands.

New Covenant in the New Testament

The New Testament begins with the account of Jesus' life, death, and resurrection. This marks the start of God's new covenant with His people. In a covenant, each side is required to do something in exchange for something else. I call the new covenant the Divine Exchange.

In the Divine Exchange, we are required to follow two, new commands. These new commands are found in Romans 10:9-10:

1. Confess with your mouth that Jesus is Lord.
2. Believe in your heart that God has raised Him from the dead.

That is it - confess and believe. In exchange for following these commands, God forgives all of our sins and gives us eternal life. On top of that, we receive the righteousness of God by way of the Holy Spirit that comes down from heaven and takes up residence within us.

Wow! What an exchange!

Life in the Spirit

It is nearly impossible to make a rule for every possible situation. And, God doesn't want us to be legalistic Pharisees obsessed with the letter of the law. Instead, He wants us to rely on Him for help and guidance. That is why He gave us the Holy Spirit. The Holy Spirit convicts us of right and wrong and gives us wisdom in difficult circumstances.

With the Holy Spirit inside of us, we are called to be transformed by the renewing of our minds. And we are to grow in holiness and righteousness. The Holy Spirit also acts as our conscience, convicting us to confess and repent any time that we sin.[13]

Finally, the Holy Spirit helps us follow Jesus' last command to His disciples: "Go and make disciples of all nations, baptizing them in the name of the Father and of the Son and of the Holy Spirit, and teaching them to obey everything I have commanded you" (Matthew 28:19-20). The Holy Spirit emboldens us to share the Good News of the Father and Son's great love for us.

The most practical way to do this is explained in the next line of *Love In A Tweet:* "Love others as ourselves." When we are so filled with God's love that it overflows into how we love others, then we are spreading the Good News through our very lives.14 We'll go more into detail about how to do that in the next chapter.

In conclusion, we are called to love God above everything and show it with unwavering obedience. This love includes:

- Loving God above anyone and anything else passionately and affectionately
- Keeping God's commands
- Confessing Jesus as Lord and believing in our hearts that He was raised from the dead
- Transforming our lives by renewing our minds
- Confessing and repenting of our sins

Action Items:
1)   Do you love God above everything? If there's an idol in your life that you've put ahead of God, confess and ask for forgiveness. Commit to loving God with your whole heart, soul, mind, and strength.

2)   Did any of the Old or New Testament laws we discussed stand out to you? That could have been the Holy Spirit prompting you to make some changes in your life. Go back and read through the 10 Commandments and Divine Exchange sections and talk to God about whatever He reveals to you.

CHAPTER 4

Love Others

Love!
Love God above everything! Show it with unwavering obedience.
Love!
Love others as yourself! Show it by living a holy and righteous life.
-Love In A Tweet

If you really keep the royal law found in Scripture, "Love your neighbor as yourself," you are doing right.
- James 2:8

In the last chapter, we discussed loving God above everything and showing it with unwavering obedience. This is truly God's will for our lives. Human beings were created to glorify and honor God in our thoughts, words, and deeds.

But how do we do this on a practical, daily level? One simple but profound method is to start each morning by declaring your "Plan For Today:"

Today, I will love the Lord my God with all my heart and with all my soul and with all my mind and with all my strength by keeping his commands. Today I will love others as I love myself by treating them the way I want to be treated.

These two commands come directly from the Holy Bible, and it is worthy to read God's message to us again:

"And you shall love the Lord your God with all your heart, with all your soul, with all your mind, and with all your strength.' This is the first commandment. And the second, like it, is this: 'You shall love your neighbor as yourself.' There is no other commandment greater than these" (Mark 12:30-31).

If you recite your "Plan For Today" every morning, you'll notice a shift in your mindset and behavior. You'll begin to view your interactions with others as opportunities to share God's love. In other words, you will be living out the second part of *Love In A Tweet*, "Love! Love others as yourself! Show it by living a holy and righteous life."

Let's dive a little deeper into what it means to love your neighbor as yourself.

Your neighbor

Many people, like myself, have asked, "Who is my neighbor?"

Thankfully, Jesus answered this question in The Parable of the Good Samaritan (see Luke 10:29-37). In this story, a man is beaten and left for dead. Then, a Samaritan shows that man great mercy by helping him. Jesus says that the Samaritan was the injured man's neighbor.

Look carefully at what happened: A person encountered a stranger in dire need. He showed mercy to the person in need. With that act of mercy, they became neighbors.

A neighborhood could be defined as the interaction of two people. Any two people who interact with each other are neighbors. Therefore, the command is to love everybody that you encounter.

Your enemy is your neighbor - love your enemy! (See Matthew 5:44)

The needy are your neighbors - be kind to them! (See Proverbs 14:31)

Everyone is your neighbor - do good to all people! (See Galatians 6:10)

As yourself

Why does Jesus say to love your neighbor as yourself? Those last two words, "as yourself," have intrigued me for many years. As I've poured over scripture and studied these verses, I've reached three conclusions:

1)   We must love what God loves. God loves us. So, we have to love ourselves.

2)   We cannot truly love anyone else if we do not love ourselves. We must be filled with wisdom and understanding about love before we can begin sharing it with others.

3)   We can learn a lot by comparing this command to the Golden Rule, "Do to others as you would have them do to you" (Matthew 7:12). Then we see that "as yourself" can mean "as you would have them do to you."

Mark 12:31	Love your neighbor	as yourself.
Matthew 7:12	Do to others	what you would have them do to you.

This simplifies the command. If you don't like people to be cruel to you, then don't be cruel to others. It is the most practical of practical guidelines.

Now that we've thoroughly discussed what it means to "love others as yourself," we'll move on to the last sentence in the tweet: "Show it by living a holy and righteous life." The three main words we'll focus on are "living," "holy," and "righteous."

How you live reveals your nature

Look at the Golden Rule in Matthew 7:12 again: "Do to others what you would have them do to you." "What you would have them do" is another way to say "what you want." But different people want different things, according to their natures. So, your nature is the yardstick against which you must measure everything.

Many years ago, someone told me a great little story that has stuck with me till today.

A frog and a scorpion were sitting on the edge of a river. Both wanted to cross to the other side. The scorpion couldn't swim, so he asked to ride on the frog's back across the river.

The frog flatly refused and said, "Why would I want to do that? You will sting me!"

The scorpion brought logic into play and said, "Why would I sting you? Surely, I love life and I don't want to die! I know that if I sting you we both will die. I am not that stupid!"

After pondering the wisdom of the scorpion's answer, the frog agreed to the scorpion's request, and off they went. In the middle of the river, the scorpion stung the frog. The frog, in his dying moments, looked back at the scorpion and asked, "Why?"

The scorpion answered, "Because it is in my nature…"

Our nature, therefore, determines how we will "do to others." If our nature is wicked, we will do wicked things. If our nature is righteous, we will do righteous things.

So, we must develop a righteous nature so that we can become holy.
Then, our righteous nature will compel us to love others and treat our neighbors as ourselves.

How can you become holy?

It will be very difficult, if not impossible, to follow the Golden Rule if we don't have a nature of holiness. Or at least, if we don't strive to be holy.

Peter makes no qualms about this, "But just as he who called you is holy, so be holy in all you do; for it is written: "Be holy, because I am holy" (1 Peter 1:15-16).

We will only become perfectly holy when Jesus Christ comes again. But we are not just stagnantly waiting. There is work to be done in this in-between time. We must be transformed into holier people through the renewing of our minds.[1]

How can I be righteous if I'm a sinner?

We all received God's righteousness when we were reborn. It was part of the "Divine Exchange" - Jesus took on our sins and we took on God's righteousness.

Does that mean that we are righteous by nature? Of course not! We are sinful by nature: "If we claim to be without sin, we deceive ourselves and the truth is not in us" (1 John 1:8).

When we were reborn, God made us righteous.[2] At that moment, all our past sins were forgiven and we were given a clean slate. On top of that, we received the Holy Spirit to guide us on how to remain righteous.

But all of us have sinned - intentionally, unintentionally, or because of ignorance - since the day of our rebirth. So, what do we do? Do we have to be reborn again? No, we must confess and repent. Then, once again, we are forgiven and receive the righteousness of God.

Show it by living a holy and righteous life

This is our challenge. How do we live a holy and righteous life?

Stating it differently, how do we become so holy and righteous that it becomes part of our nature?

Here is some helpful advice from God's word:

1. **Listen to the righteousness of God.** We received this righteousness when we were reborn. It is in us, we just have to follow it. We all basically know what is

'right' and what is 'wrong' - the distinction or ability to discern was given to us free of charge. Let your conscience guide you.[3]

2. **Ask God for guidance.** God sent the Holy Spirit to dwell within us. He is with us 24/7 and we only need to ask if we are not sure. He answers us.[4]

3. **Discover it in His Word.** "Man shall not live on bread alone, but on every word that comes from the mouth of God" (Matthew 4:4). "Blessed rather are those who hear the word of God and obey it" (Luke 11:28).

Once again I'd like to share Paul's prayer for us:

"And this is my prayer: that your love may abound more and more in knowledge and depth of insight so that you may be able to discern what is best and may be pure and blameless for the day of Christ" (Philippians 1:9-10).

This prayer is central to understanding God's love and our response to it. These verses teach us that:

1.   We must grow in our knowledge of God's love, mercy, and grace.
2.   Then we will be able to discern what is best.
3.   God will purify us to be ready for Christ's return.

We've now gone into great detail and shared the scriptural backing for the *Love In A Tweet:*

Love!
Love God above everything! Show it with unwavering obedience.
Love!
Love others as yourself! Show it by living a holy and righteous life.

In the next section, we will discuss the practical ways that we can love God, ourselves, and others in our daily lives. We'll also give simple examples of what it means to walk in obedience and live a holy and righteous life.

Action Items:

1)   Write down the "Plan For Today" at the beginning of this chapter and place it in your Bible or journal. You can even use it as a bookmark. Commit to reading this plan at the start of each day.

2)   Think about all the people you interacted with in the last 24 hours. Did you treat them as you would have wanted to be treated? Ask God to help you be more loving each day.

"Whoever pursues righteousness and love finds life, prosperity and honor"
- Proverbs 21:21

CHAPTER 5

Living a Life of Love

I'm not sure if it's old age or just a sign of the times, but it seems as though life is rushing past like a roaring river with too many rapids to negotiate.

We get up in the morning, rush to get ready for work, rush to work, rush through the day, rush to get home, and, before we know it, we rush off to bed. Then we just start all over the next day.

Rushing blurs our vision regarding what is truly important. We become so focused on meeting deadlines and crossing items off lists that we forget about God and His commands. We don't realize that a lot of what matters so much to us in this world will be declared "Utterly meaningless!" in the next (Ecclesiastes 1:2).

This book has focused on loving God, ourselves, and others. You may have been very convicted about needing to be more loving. But, if you are not paying attention, you will rush right past opportunities to love God and love your neighbor as yourself.

Living a life of love is countercultural. It requires us to slow down and be intentional with how we treat others. Love can't be rushed. And we can't grow in love through sheer force of will or wishful thinking.

In order to live a life of love, we need wisdom and the Holy Spirit. These are some of the good gifts that our loving Father longs to give us.1 So we must ask, seek, and knock, presenting God with our request to grow in wisdom and learn to follow the Holy Spirit.2

After asking God for help living a life of love, we should also turn to the Bible for guidance. The Bible has a lot to teach us about wisdom and will also help us tune our ears to the Holy Spirit.

If we turn to God's Word and listen for guidance from the indwelling Spirit, we will find the wisdom to discern what is good (loving) and what is wicked (unloving). In this way, wisdom and the Holy Spirit will teach us how to live with love.

Scour Proverbs for Wisdom

Proverbs is a great source of wisdom. It is attributed to King Solomon who was the son of King David. In 2 Chronicles 1, God appeared to Solomon and said, "Ask for whatever you want me to give you." Solomon asked God for wisdom and God promised it to him. That wisdom is available to us by way of the Book of Proverbs.

There is so much wisdom in Proverbs that every time I finish it, I just want to read it again! When I realized that the book has 31 chapters, I committed to reading through it every month. I'm so grateful for the ways that God teaches me about wisdom in Proverbs.

These three profound statements grab my attention each time that I read Proverbs:

> "The beginning of wisdom is this: Get wisdom. Though it cost all you have, get understanding" (Proverbs 4:7).

> "The fear of the Lord is the beginning of wisdom, and knowledge of the Holy One is understanding" (Proverbs 9:10).

> "Whoever pursues righteousness and love finds life, prosperity and honor" (Proverbs 21:21).

Our culture equates growing older with becoming wiser. However, that is not always the case. These verses remind me that becoming wise requires sacrifice, a deeper knowledge of God, and the pursuit of righteousness. Therefore, wisdom is not the fruit of old age, but rather the fruit of persistently seeking to grow in wisdom.

Proverbs provides wisdom about righteousness: What to be and what to do.
For example:
- Trust in the Lord
- Guard your heart
- Hold your tongue

Proverbs provides wisdom about wickedness: What not to be and what to not do.
For example:
- Don't be wise in your own eyes
- Don't envy the violent
- Don't commit adultery

Sometimes the wisdom of God is very straightforward and easy to understand. But other times, it is hidden and we must truly seek it. We've all faced situations that are in the "gray areas" of life where right and wrong (or loving and unloving actions) were not easily discernible.

Those are the moments when we must truly hit our knees, begging God to give us wisdom on how to move forward. If we already have the wisdom of Proverbs in our minds at those moments, it will make that discerning process much easier.

To simulate how we must seek wisdom, I've made a type of seek-and-find exercise. Hidden below are phrases from Proverbs that point to righteousness and others that point to wickedness. Circle or underline the ones that provide wisdom about righteousness:

Gossip, trustworthiness, kindness, cruelty, perverse hearts, blameless ways, generosity, the fruit of our lips, lying tongue, speaking rashly, happy hearts, bribes, life-giving correction, committing what we do to the Lord, pride, desire without knowledge, laziness, kindness to the poor, being hot-tempered, strife, curses one's father or mother, humility, borrowing, injustice, oppressing or exploiting the poor, being skilled, gluttony, prudence, being blameless, concealing of sins, working, stinginess, defending the rights of the poor and needy.

*Answers in Annexure E

There are whole books on the wisdom of Proverbs, and there is no way that we can unpack all of it here. That is why reading through Proverbs on a regular basis is so beneficial.

However, I want to point out just one more passage that is relevant to our pursuit of loving God well. Proverbs 6:16-19 mentions seven things that God hates or that are detestable to Him. We must avoid these actions and character traits if we want to love God as He wants to be loved:

- Haughty eyes (pride)
- A lying tongue
- Hands that shed innocent blood
- A heart that devises wicked schemes
- Feet that are quick to rush into evil
- A false witness who pours out lies
- A person who stirs up conflict

Regularly reading Proverbs will help us grow in wisdom and live a life of love. When we face difficult decisions, the wisdom of this book will help us make more loving, God-honoring choices. Ultimately, growing in wisdom will shape our very nature, making it easier to love God, ourselves, and others.

Bear the Fruit of the Spirit

We've talked about the Holy Spirit a few times in this book. As a reminder:

- In Chapter 1, we referred to the characteristics of God, which include "God is three-in-one, God the Father, God the Son, and God the Holy Spirit."

- In Chapter 2, we posed the question "How do I love others?" One of the answers was that we can rely on the Holy Spirit to help us make loving choices.

- In Chapter 3, we read about how the Holy Spirit acts as our conscience, which helps us show love with unwavering obedience.

- In Chapter 4, we discussed how the Holy Spirit helps us to live righteously.

Living a life of love requires that we are in tune with the Holy Spirit. We know this, we've read about it, and we believe it. But what do we do about it? How can we learn to identify and respond to the Spirit's prompting in our lives?

I used to be a bit skeptical and a tad envious of people who regularly said things like, "God told me this," or "I sensed God leading me to do that." They seemed so in tune with the Spirit, while I felt rather lost and confused.

So, as we are getting into the practical ways to love God and love others, we need to learn some practical ways to tune our ears to the Holy Spirit. His guidance and wisdom are necessary for living a life of love.

One powerful way that I've found to tune my ears to the Spirit is by growing the fruits of the Spirit. As I seek to grow in these character traits, I know the Spirit will sow them in my heart and help them to grow. Throughout that process, I'll learn to notice the Spirit's activity in my life more and more.

The fruits of the Spirit are listed in Galatians 5:22-23. Take a few moments to prayerfully consider how much your life reflects these characteristics. Then rank them using this scale:

1= Good   2= Okay   3= Needs Improvement

Love		Goodness	
Joy		Faithfulness	
Peace		Gentleness	
Patience		Self-Control	
Kindness		Overall	

Now ask God how He wants you to work on all of the 3s that you marked. Really sit with this question for a while. Then write down whatever God instructed you to do.

Have the mindset of Christ Jesus

This book has provided quite a few guidelines for you to study and meditate on, guidelines on how to live a life of love by becoming righteous and holy - like Jesus. Yet, none of this will be possible if you don't have the mindset of Jesus.

In Philippians 2, the Apostle Paul gives us a small window into Jesus' mindset:

-        Jesus Christ is God, yet He came to earth to make Himself nothing and to adopt the nature of a servant.

-        Jesus Christ is God, yet He humbled Himself by becoming obedient to death on the cross.

The Apostle Paul also instructs us to have the same mindset as Christ Jesus in our relationships with each other (Philippians 2:5). If our minds are set on trying to master others or exalt ourselves over others, then we are not living a life of love.

So, let the Holy Spirit guide you to have the mindset of Christ Jesus, a mindset of servitude and humility.

Then, and only then, will you be able to face Christ every day and on His day as blameless and pure as children of God without fault in a warped and crooked generation. Then you will shine like stars in the sky as you hold firmly to the word of life. And then you will be able to boast on the day of Christ that you did not run or labor in vain (Phillippians 2:15-16).

Encouragement

Take a moment to assess how you feel about the fruits of the spirit that you marked as a "3." There is a human tendency to beat ourselves up for our imperfections. Instead, you can take these as opportunities for growth. It can be exciting to imagine how much better life will be when you are more patient and kind.

In the next chapter, we will be doing more grading and assessing ourselves. Sometimes changing habits and striving for holiness seems overwhelming. In those moments, I encourage you to read and re-read 2 Peter 1:3-11:

His divine power has given us everything we need for a godly life through our knowledge of him who called us by his own glory and goodness. Through these he has given us his very great and precious promises, so that through them you may participate in the divine nature, having escaped the corruption in the world caused by evil desires (v. 3-4).

You are not in this alone. God is with you, providing his divine power, glory, and goodness to help you along the way. And your struggle is not in vain. God has promised that you can participate in the divine nature!

For this very reason, make every effort to add to your faith goodness; and to goodness, knowledge; and to knowledge, self-control; and to self-control, perseverance; and to perseverance, godliness; and to godliness, mutual affection; and to mutual affection, love. For if you possess these qualities in increasing measure... you will never stumble, and you will receive a rich welcome into the eternal kingdom of our Lord and Savior Jesus Christ (v. 5-8a,10b-11).

Can you see how growth is a process of transformation? You start with faith and then add goodness and keep growing in holy attributes and increasing in godly qualities throughout your time here on earth. So that you are ready for Christ's second coming and your wonderful reception and life in heaven for all eternity.

Action Items:

1)   Commit to reading through Proverbs at a regular interval. This could be one chapter a day, which would get you through the book in a month. Or it could be at another frequency that works better for you. Make the commitment and share it with someone who can hold you accountable to it.

2)   Write down the fruits that you ranked as a 3 on a sticky note. Put that sticky note somewhere that you'll see daily, such as the mirror, your computer, or the steering wheel of your car. Every time you see that sticky note, pray for God to grow those fruits in your life and make you more in tune with the Holy Spirit.

CHAPTER 6

Transformation and Renewal

Be transformed by the renewing of your mind.
- Romans 12:2

Over the last 5 chapters, we have learned a lot about God's love. We've seen that His love is perfect and that the ultimate expression of God's love will be letting us spend eternity with Him in heaven.

God's great love stirs up a deep response from us. We want to love God as He deserves to be loved. We want to honor God by living a life of love.[1] But, it's not easy.

God's love is perfect. Ours is imperfect. God is sinless. We are sinners. Perhaps we feel like Isaiah when he said, "All of us have become like one who is unclean, and all our righteous acts are like filthy rags; we all shrivel up like a leaf, and like the wind our sins sweep us away" (Isaiah 64:6).

But Isaiah didn't give up, so neither should we. Transformation is possible! Just listen to this Biblical encouragement:

-	"Do not conform to the pattern of this world, but be transformed by the renewing of your mind. Then you will be able to test and approve what God's will is—his good, pleasing and perfect will (Romans 12:2)."

-	"And we all, who with unveiled faces contemplate the Lord's glory, are being transformed into his image with ever-increasing glory, which comes from the Lord, who is the Spirit" (2 Corinthians 3:18).

Together, these verses teach us that the source of our transformation is "the Lord, who is the Spirit," but we must also do our part by renewing our minds and contemplating the Lord's glory.

God has taught me a lot about transformation over the past year. It started when I committed to reading the Bible daily. As my hunger for scripture grew, so did my hunger to be transformed into God's image. The more I listened to God's word, the more I began to hear the Spirit's promptings in my daily life.

One of the first things the Spirit revealed to me was that I was slow to listen and quick to anger. I knew that was in direct contrast to what God wants from me. So, I began praying for God to change me. Every time I realized that I was angry, I reached out to God for help. And slowly, God is changing my character.

The pattern of my transformation was:
1)   The Bible revealed how my nature differed from the nature God wants from me. [2]
2)   I started to ask, seek, and knock for God to change me. [3]
3)   The Holy Spirit slowly but surely affected the change. [4]

Wisdom Prayer
Something else that helped with my transformation was the Wisdom Prayer. I wrote this prayer and began reciting it each morning. It was my daily plea for transformation.

Wisdom Prayer

God, grant me the Wisdom
To know what I should change,
Power to bring the change to fulfilment,
And Faith to know that You have blessed it.

This prayer was inspired by the Serenity Prayer, which is something that I've turned to throughout my life. The Serenity Prayer reminds us that many things are outside of our control. The Wisdom Prayer teaches us that transformation is possible. They are both powerful prayers to commit to memory and use regularly.

Serenity Prayer

God, grant me the Serenity
To accept the things I cannot change...
Courage to change the things I can,
And Wisdom to know the difference.

- Reinhold Niebuhr

The Checklist for Change
Once I realized how God was using the Bible to affect change in my life, I started to keep a list of the traits God wants in His followers. Over the past year, I've read the entire Bible twice, including the New Testament five times, and Proverbs twelve times. With each pass through the scriptures, I've combed out and written down traits of holy people.

I identified 38 traits of a holy person. I examined my own heart and tried to see which of the traits I needed to improve. Then, I realized that I needed a second set of eyes.

So, I asked my wife, "Beatrice, do you think I'm honest?" There was no hesitation. She gave me a resounding, "Yes!" Then I asked if I was humble. There was an uncomfortable silence, and I knew I needed to work on my humility.

Every trait that I needed to improve on was added to my Change List. It became my daily prayer for God to help me change those traits. And, slowly, I'm transforming!

I'd like to share my Checklist for Change with you, but it's important that you realize that this is merely a tool. God is the one who brings the change. I pray that God will use this simple exercise to illuminate the areas of your life where He would like to bring transformation.

Go through the list below and compare each trait side-by-side. Put an X next to the word that more accurately describes you. For example, are you more affectionate or unfeeling? Put an X next to that trait then move to the next line.

Many people struggle to judge themselves accurately. So it may help to ask your partner or a close friend to assist you with this. However, this "judging" should not be undertaken with a spirit of condemnation but rather of hopeful anticipation of the wonderful changes that God will bring to your life.

If you need more explanation or want to see the biblical references for each of these traits, refer to Annexure D.

Checklist for Change
Now, write down any of the traits in the last column that you put an X next to. This is your Change List!

Am I more	like this	OR	like this?
	Affectionate		Unfeeling
	Agreeable		Disagreeable
	Blameless		Blameworthy
	Calm		Anxious
	Cheerful		Grumbling
	Comforting		Distressing
	Considerate		Inconsiderate
	Content		Dissatisfied

Am I more	like this	OR	like this?
	Empathetic		Insensitive
	Faithful		Disloyal
	Forgiving		Vindictive
	Generous		Stingy
	Gentle		Harsh
	Godly		Worldly
	Honest		Dishonest
	Hopeful		Cynical
	Humble		Proud
	Joyful		Miserable
	Kind		Cruel
	Loving		Hateful
	Merciful		Ruthless
	Modest		Boastful
	Patient		Impatient
	Peaceful		Easily provoked
	Persistent		Hesitant
	Positive		Pessimistic
	Protective		Negligent
	Respectful		Disrespectful
	Righteous		Wicked
	Self-Controlled		Easily Provoked
	Selfless		Selfish
	Sincere		Insincere
	Sympathetic		Unsympathetic
	Tolerant		Intolerant
	Trustworthy		Unreliable
	Truthful		Deceitful
	Wise		Foolish

Begin asking God how He wants you to tackle the traits in your Change List. Pray for the Holy Spirit to make you aware of opportunities to grow and change those traits. Check back in with the list regularly, trusting that God will bring about the change that you seek. Remember that this is not a test or a source of judgement. You are growing in these traits to express your great love for God and see His transformation at work in your life.

Force-Field Analysis

Another tool that can guide your transformation is the Force-Field Analysis. In this exercise, you will compare where you are now to where you want to be. Then you will evaluate what is holding you back from reaching your goal and what is propelling you towards it. In the end, you'll have a helpful visual representation of the change needed in your life.

How to do a Force-Field Analysis:

1) Draw a horizontal line in the middle of a blank piece of paper. Label this: My Current Nature.

2) Draw a horizontal line at the top of the paper. Label this: Holiness.

3) **Withholding Force:** Think about what forces work against your ability to be holy. What is holding you back? These may be some of the items you identified on your Change List. Draw downward arrows from the Holiness Line to the My Current Nature Line. Label each one with the forces that hold you back.

4) **Missing Force:** What could help propel you closer to holiness? These are things currently missing from your life that you know would be helpful to have. Draw arrows upwards from below the My Current Nature Line to represent each of those forces.

Once this little exercise is completed, the task at hand is simply to remove the withholding forces and institute the missing forces.

For example, from your checklist, you may identify that you are quite impatient. That is a Withholding Force, and it must be removed.

From your checklist, you may find that you don't really think about the needs of others. That is an indication of a Missing Force that you may want to place on the list of things to start doing.

When I first embarked on this exercise, I ended up with a long list of both Withholding Forces and Missing Forces. This list included:

- Regular and consistent time with God in His Word (Missing Force)
- Regular and consistent communion as part of His body - attending Church on Sundays (Missing Force)
- Impatience (Withholding Force)
- Humility (Withholding Force)
- And the list goes on and on…

I am still "on it" and some changes are easier than others. When it gets difficult, I remember the Divine Exchange. I think about how God gave me salvation, eternal life, His righteousness, and His Spirit. My deep gratitude and desire to please Him spur me on to seek transformation and renewal.

RISE with God

In 2 Peter 1:5-7, we're told to add seven characteristics to our faith: goodness, knowledge, self-control, perseverance, godliness, mutual affection, and love. We've discussed most of these character traits in this book. But now we will focus on self-control.

This is a technique I learned in 1987 while attending a course at the University of Colorado. It was originally used to help people learn to deal with conflict. This powerful tool will help you moderate your responses and increase your self-control.

I've adjusted the original technique slightly to apply it to our spiritual lives. RISE with God is a way to harness the power of our minds for good. Satan often uses our minds to trick us into straying from the narrow path. This technique will help thwart his attacks.

The psychology behind this tool comes from Viktor Frankl's paramount discovery that:

"Between stimulus and response, man has the freedom to choose."

This is how our minds work: 1) A wicked thought crosses our minds. 2) We formulate a reaction to it. 3) We react.

What if we could elongate that second step? Then we could properly evaluate our intended reaction and see if it is holy or not. With a longer second step, we could choose not to act on our initial, sinful impulse. We could make a holier choice.

Here is the technique:
Imagine a little helicopter with only two seats - one for God and one for you.

Sit back, close your eyes, and see the little helicopter in your mind's eye. What colour is it? Is it round or oblong? How big is it? How long is its tail? What kind of chairs does it have and what does the dashboard look like?

Do you see your little helicopter? Now start it and make it available to take off at all times.

When a negative thought crosses your mind, jump into your helicopter and RISE. This will stop your natural thought process. You will get away from everything as you RISE.

R = Relax
I = Internal Reaction
S = Situation Analyses
E = Engage wisely

Here's an example of this technique in action:

Someone calls you a fool. Your natural response is to insult them right back. But instead, you use this as a stimulus to kick off a helicopter ride. You RELAX and let go of your emotions. If you are still tempted to snap back in anger, play that out in an INTERNAL REACTION. This is like shouting it out without opening your mouth.

Now you do a SITUATION ANALYSIS. Ask God if He would have approved of your intended response. Ask yourself how Jesus would have responded to the situation. Ask what a holy or righteous response would be.

This process may take only a few seconds, but it is critical that you get into that space between stimulus and response. That space is where you choose how to respond with guidance from God.

Finish your helicopter ride by descending, getting out, and responding to the negative stimulus as God instructed you to. This is how you ENGAGE WISELY.

Between stimulus and response, God will show you how to respond!

This technique has brought me great joy and freedom. I am no longer a slave to my reactive nature. I can make wiser choices and turn to God in the midst of difficult situations. And so I encourage you to…

RISE with God when you get angry.
RISE with God when you are tempted.
RISE with God when you are anxious or worried.
RISE with God always!

CHAPTER 7

Love and Love

Do you yearn for better things? Does your heart long for its true home?

That is a sure sign that you are drawing closer to God and He is increasing your hunger for heaven. You are sensing paradise drawing nearer day by day. And you can almost see it, hear it, touch it, smell it, and taste it.

Your faith journey began when you were born again. And its ultimate goal is to spend eternity with God. But now you are in the in-between time.

And so you strive forward, running with perseverance the race towards eternity with God.[1] You keep your eyes fixed on Jesus in eager anticipation of His second coming and in deep gratitude that His blood washed your sins away and bought you the free gift of salvation.

When you first confessed Christ as Lord and believed in your heart that He was resurrected from the dead, God clothed you in a white robe of His righteousness. Yet, the road between being born again and reaching heaven's gates is a long and winding one. And you are traveling this journey as a fallible human being, prone to blemishing your white robe.

So you seek to obey God's commands, follow in the ways of Christ, and rely more and more on the guidance of the Holy Spirit.

You know that God has called you to run your race toward paradise with love:

"Love the Lord your God with all your heart and with all your soul and with all your mind and with all your strength. Love your neighbor as yourself."
- Mark 12:30-31

You believe that God is love and that loving God involves keeping His commandments:

Love!
Love God above everything! Show it with unwavering obedience.
- Love In A Tweet

You understand that God calls you to love yourself and others and show that love in all you do:

Love!
Love others as yourself! Show it by living a holy and righteous life.
- Love In A Tweet

Love and Love! We are commanded to not only feel love for God and others but to show it. God showed His love for us, and He expects us to show our love for Him and others.[2]

Love boils up from our Spirit-filled souls and manifests itself along our journey to paradise in the form of works and deeds that glorify God. Such God-pleasing actions can only come from a holy and righteous soul.[3] These are signs of the transformation and renewal that God has called us to.

Growing in love requires conscientious and persistent work. The main tools of this effort are prayer, reading the Bible, and Christian fellowship. And in this book, you've found other helpful tools such as the Plan For Today, the Wisdom Prayer, the Checklist for Change, and learning how to RISE with God.

Are you living a life of love? Hopefully, this book has helped you answer that question. And, perhaps it even brought you new questions, such as "Am I growing in love?" "Am I being renewed and transformed into a more loving person?" and "Have I thanked God for His love today?"

The motivators and personal development gurus of the world all tell us that success starts with a clearly defined goal. Christians, true Christians, set this as their goal:

To be pure and blameless for the day of Christ.

I am leaving you with one of the most powerful and important prayers that you can ever pray.
Dear Lord, this is my prayer:
That my love may abound more and more in knowledge and depth of insight so that I may be able to discern what is best and may be pure and blameless for the day of Christ.
In Jesus' name. Amen.[4]

This prayer is all about
- Love
- Growth
- Insight into God's will
- Discernment between right and wrong
- Transformation, renewal, and change

This prayer is a way of preparing for the second coming of Jesus Christ when God's Plan will be fulfilled and He will say. "It is done."

I start every day with the Prayer above, and then I state my Plan For Today.

MY PLAN FOR TODAY

"Today, I will love the Lord my God with all my heart and with all my soul and with all my mind and with all my strength by keeping his commands. Today I will also love others as I love myself by doing what I would have them do to me."

In closing, may I end where we started. In the very beginning, I quoted Proverbs 8:17-18:

I love those who love me,
and those who seek me find me.
With me are riches and honor,
enduring wealth and prosperity.

Finding God while living a life of love is rewarding, not only when Christ returns but every day until then. It is a life that will be filled with riches, honor, enduring wealth, and prosperity.

May God bless you and keep you, make His face shine on you, be gracious to you, turn His face toward you and give you peace on your journey of love.

Annexures

Annexure A: God is...
This is referenced in Chapter 1.

Love
* "And so we know and rely on the love God has for us. God is love. Whoever lives in love lives in God, and God in them" (1 John 4:16).

Wisdom
* "Let the name of God be praised forever and ever, for wisdom and power belong to him (Daniel 2:20)."

Knowable
* "The Son is the radiance of God's glory and the representation of His essence" (Hebrews 1:3).
* "No one has ever seen God, but the one and only Son, who is himself God and is in closest relationship with the Father, has made him known" (John 1:18).

Three in one: God the Father, God the Son (Jesus Christ), and God the Holy Spirit
* "Therefore go and make disciples of all nations, baptizing them in the name of the Father and of the Son and of the Holy Spirit" (Matthew 28:19).
* "But the Advocate, the Holy Spirit, whom the Father will send in my name, will teach you all things and will remind you of everything I have said to you" (John 14:26).

God is spirit
* "Now to the King eternal, immortal, invisible, the only God, be honor and glory for ever and ever. Amen" (1 Timothy 1:17).
* "God is spirit, and his worshipers must worship in the Spirit and in truth" (John 4:24).

From Everlasting to Everlasting
* "His dominion is an everlasting dominion that will not pass away, and his kingdom is one that will never be destroyed" (Daniel 7:14).
* "Do you not know? Have you not heard? The Lord is the everlasting God, the Creator of the ends of the earth. He will not grow tired or weary ,and his understanding no one can fathom" (Isaiah 40:28).

Immutable (unchanging over time or unable to be changed)
- "Every good and perfect gift is from above, coming down from the Father of the heavenly lights, who does not change like shifting shadows" (James 1:17).

Able to do anything
- "Jesus looked at them and said, 'With man this is impossible, but not with God; all things are possible with God.'"(Mark 10:27).

Perfect in knowledge, He knows everything
- "Great is our Lord and mighty in power; his understanding has no limit" (Psalm 147:5).

With us
- "What, then, shall we say in response to these things? If God is for us, who can be against us?" (Romans 8:31)
- "...the Spirit of truth. The world cannot accept him, because it neither sees him nor knows him. But you know him, for he lives with you and will be in you" (John 14:17).

Sovereign
- "...God, the blessed and only Ruler, the King of kings and Lord of lords" (1 Timothy 6:15).

Holy
- "Such a high priest truly meets our need—one who is holy, blameless, pure, set apart from sinners, exalted above the heavens" (Hebrews 7:26).

Just
- "The Lord is just in all his actions and exhibits love in all he does" (Psalm 145:17).
- "Righteousness and justice are the foundation of your throne;
- love and faithfulness go before you." (Psalm 89:14).

Graceful
- "Let us then approach God's throne of grace with confidence, so that we may receive mercy and find grace to help us in our time of need" (Hebrews 4:16).

Merciful
- "The Lord is compassionate and gracious, slow to anger, abounding in love" (Psalm 103:8).
- Mercy: compassion or forgiveness shown toward someone whom it is within one's power to punish or harm.[1]

Slow to anger
- "The Lord is compassionate and gracious, slow to anger, abounding in love" (Psalm 103:8).

Wrathful
- "Let no one deceive you with empty words, for because of such things God's wrath comes on those who are disobedient" (Ephesians 5:6).

Good
- "Praise the Lord, for the Lord is good. Sing praises to his name, for it is pleasant" (Psalm 135:3).
- "Now this is the gospel message we have heard from him and announce to you: God is light, and in him there is no darkness at all" (1 John 1:5).
- "For the LORD is good; His lovingkindness is everlasting, and His faithfulness to all generations" (Psalm 100:5).
- "Why do you call me good?" Jesus answered. "No one is good—except God alone" (Luke 18:18).

Forgiving
- "For I will be merciful toward their evil deeds, and their sins I will remember no longer" (Hebrews 8:12).
- "In him we have redemption through his blood, the forgiveness of sins, in accordance with the riches of God's grace" (Ephesians 1:7).

Jealous
- "For you must not worship any other god, for the Lord, whose name is Jealous, is a jealous God" (Exodus 34:14).

Truthful
- "And we know that the Son of God has come and has given us insight to know him who is true, and we are in him who is true, in his Son Jesus Christ. This one is the true God and eternal life. Little children, guard yourselves from idols" (1 John 5:20-21).

Faithful
- "...if we are faithless, he remains faithful, for he cannot disown himself" (2 Timothy 2:13).
- "Lord, you are my God; I will exalt you and praise your name, for in perfect faithfulness you have done wonderful things, things planned long ago" (Isaiah 25:1).

Glorious
- "And the God of all grace, who called you to his eternal glory in Christ, after you have suffered a little while, will himself restore you and make you strong, firm and steadfast" (1 Peter 5:10).

- "For you know that we dealt with each of you as a father deals with his own children, encouraging, comforting and urging you to live lives worthy of God, who calls you into his kingdom and glory" (1 Thessalonians 2:11-13).

Annexure B: The Commandments

The Ten Commandments
Exodus 20:1-17

And God spoke all these words:
"I am the Lord your God, who brought you out of Egypt, out of the land of slavery.

"You shall have no other gods before me.

"You shall not make for yourself an image in the form of anything in heaven above or on the earth beneath or in the waters below. You shall not bow down to them or worship them; for I, the Lord your God, am a jealous God, punishing the children for the sin of the parents to the third and fourth generation of those who hate me, but showing love to a thousand generations of those who love me and keep my commandments.

"You shall not misuse the name of the Lord your God, for the Lord will not hold anyone guiltless who misuses his name.

"Remember the Sabbath day by keeping it holy. Six days you shall labor and do all your work, but the seventh day is a sabbath to the Lord your God. On it you shall not do any work, neither you, nor your son or daughter, nor your male or female servant, nor your animals, nor any foreigner residing in your towns. For in six days the Lord made the heavens and the earth, the sea, and all that is in them, but he rested on the seventh day. Therefore the Lord blessed the Sabbath day and made it holy.

"Honor your father and your mother, so that you may live long in the land the Lord your God is giving you.

"You shall not murder.

"You shall not commit adultery.

"You shall not steal.

"You shall not give false testimony against your neighbor.

"You shall not covet your neighbor's house. You shall not covet your neighbor's wife, or his male or female servant, his ox or donkey, or anything that belongs to your neighbor."

The Greatest Commandments - Love!
Mark 12:29-31

"The most important one," answered Jesus, "is this: 'Hear, O Israel: The Lord our God, the Lord is one. Love the Lord your God with all your heart and with all your soul and with all your mind and with all your strength.' The second is this: 'Love your neighbor as yourself.'There is no commandment greater than these."

The Great Commission
Matthew 28:18-20

Then Jesus came to them and said, "All authority in heaven and on earth has been given to me. Therefore go and make disciples of all nations, baptizing them in the name of the Father and of the Son and of the Holy Spirit, and teaching them to obey everything I have commanded you. And surely I am with you always, to the very end of the age."

Confess and Believe
Romans 10:9-10

If you declare with your mouth, "Jesus is Lord," and believe in your heart that God raised him from the dead, you will be saved. For it is with your heart that you believe and are justified, and it is with your mouth that you profess your faith and are saved.

Be transformed and renew
Romans 12:2

Do not conform to the pattern of this world, but be transformed by the renewing of your mind. Then you will be able to test and approve what God's will is—his good, pleasing and perfect will.

Annexure C: The greatest is love
1 Corinthians 13

If I speak in the tongues of men or of angels, but do not have love, I am only a resounding gong or a clanging cymbal. If I have the gift of prophecy and can fathom all mysteries and all knowledge, and if I have a faith that can move mountains, but do not have love, I am nothing. If I give all I possess to the poor and give over my body to hardship that I may boast, but do not have love, I gain nothing.

Love is patient, love is kind. It does not envy, it does not boast, it is not proud. It does not dishonor others, it is not self-seeking, it is not easily angered, it keeps no record of wrongs. Love does not delight in evil but rejoices with the truth. It always protects, always trusts, always hopes, always perseveres.

Love never fails. But where there are prophecies, they will cease; where there are tongues, they will be stilled; where there is knowledge, it will pass away. For we know in part and we prophesy in part, but when completeness comes, what is in part disappears. When I was a child, I talked like a child, I thought like a child, I reasoned like a child. When I became a man, I put the ways of childhood behind me. For now we see only a reflection as in a mirror; then we shall see face to face. Now I know in part; then I shall know fully, even as I am fully known.

And now these three remain: faith, hope and love. But the greatest of these is love.

Annexure D: Checklist for Change[1]

Be affectionate: Readily feeling or showing fondness or tenderness.
- Don't be unfeeling, unsympathetic, harsh, or callous.
- 2 Peter 1:5-7

Be agreeable: Enjoyable and pleasurable; pleasant.
- Don't be disagreeable: Not pleasant or enjoyable.
- Philippians 2:14

Be blameless: Innocent of wrongdoing.
- Don't be blameworthy, responsible for wrongdoing, and deserving of censure or blame.
- 2 Peter 3:14

Be calm: Not showing or feeling nervousness, anger, or other strong emotions.
- Don't be anxious: A feeling of worry, nervousness, or unease, typically about an imminent event or something with an uncertain outcome.
- Proverbs 19:19, Matthew 6:25, Philippians 4:6

Be cheerful: Noticeably happy and optimistic.
- Don't be grumbling: Complain about something in a bad-tempered way.
- Philippians 2:14

Be comforting: Serving to alleviate a person's feelings of grief or distress.
- Don't be distressing: Causing anxiety, sorrow or pain; upsetting.
- 1 Corinthians 14:3

Be considerate: Careful not to cause inconvenience or hurt to others.
- Don't be inconsiderate: Thoughtlessly causing hurt or inconvenience to others.
- James 3:17

Be content: Accept as adequate despite wanting more or better.
- Don't be dissatisfied: Not content or happy with something.
- 1 Timothy 6:6

Be empathetic: Showing an ability to understand and share the feelings of another.
- Don't be insensitive: Showing or feeling no concern for others' feelings.
- 1 Peter 3:8, 1 John 3:17

Be encouraging: Give support, confidence, or hope.
- Don't be discouraging: Causing someone to lose confidence or enthusiasm; depressing.
- 1 Corinthians 14:3, Hebrews 10:25

Be faithful: Remaining loyal and steadfast.
- Don't be unfaithful: Disloyal, treacherous, or insincere.
- Proverbs 28:20, Matthew 25:21

Be forgiving: Willing to stop feeling resentful toward someone for an offense
- Don't be vindictive: Having or showing a strong or unreasoning desire for revenge.
- Ephesians 4:32, Matthew 6:12

Be generous: Showing a readiness to give more of something, as money or time, than is strictly necessary or expected.
- Don't be stingy: Lacking consideration for others, concerned chiefly with one's own personal profit or pleasure.
- Deuteronomy 15:10, Proverbs 11:25, Proverbs 22:9, Luke 11:41

Be gentle: Having or showing a mild, kind, or tender temperament or character.
- Don't be harsh: Inconsiderate and unkind to others.
- Ephesians 4:2, Philippians 4:5, Galatians 5:23

Be godly: Devoutly religious; pious.
- Don't be worldly: Concerned with material values or ordinary life rather than a spiritual existence.
- 2 Peter 1:5-7

Be honest: Free of deceit and untruthfulness; sincere.
- Don't be dishonest: Behaving or prone to behave in an untrustworthy or fraudulent way.
- Proverbs 22:21

Be hopeful: Feeling or inspiring optimism about a future event.
- Don't be cynical: Doubtful as to whether something will happen or whether it is worthwhile.
- Romans 12:12

Be humble: Having or showing a modest or low estimate of one's own importance.
- Don't be proud: Feeling deep pleasure or satisfaction as a result of one's own achievements, qualities, or possessions or those of someone with whom one is closely associated.
- Matthew 23:12, 1 Peter 3:8

Be joyful: Feeling, expressing, or causing great pleasure and happiness.
- Don't be miserable: Wretchedly unhappy or uncomfortable.
- Romans 12:12, Psalm 68:3

Be kind: Having or showing a friendly, generous, and considerate nature.
- Don't be cruel: Willfully causing pain or suffering to others, or feeling no concern about it.
- Ephesians 4:32

Be loving: Feeling or showing love or great care
- Don't be hateful: Feel intense or passionate dislike for someone.
- Matthew 22:36-40

Be merciful: Compassion or forgiveness shown toward someone whom it is within one's power to punish or harm.
- Don't be ruthless: Having or showing no pity or compassion for others.
- Matthew 5:7

Be modest: Unassuming or moderate in the estimation of one's abilities or achievements.
- Don't be boastful: Showing excessive pride and self-satisfaction in one's achievements, possessions, or abilities.
- 1 Corinthians 12:23

Be patient: Able to accept or tolerate delays, problems, or suffering without becoming annoyed or anxious.

- Don't be impatient: Having or showing a tendency to be quickly irritated or provoked.
- Ephesians 4:2

Be peaceful: Free from disturbance; tranquil.
- Don't be angered: Filled with anger; provoked in anger.
- Proverbs 12:20, 1 Peter 3:11

Be persistent: Continuing firmly or obstinately in a course of action in spite of difficulty or opposition.
- Don't be irresolute: Showing or feeling hesitancy; uncertain.
- 1 Corinthians 13:7, 2 Peter 1:5-7

Be positive: Constructive, optimistic, or confident.
- Don't be pessimistic: See the worst aspect of things or believe that the worst will happen.
- Romans 12:12, Romans 15:13

Be protective: Having or showing a strong wish to keep someone or something safe from harm.
- Don't be negligent: Failing to take proper care in doing something.
- 1 Corinthians 13:7

Be respectful: Regard with great respect.
- Don't be disrespectful: Showing a lack of respect or courtesy; impolite.
- 1 Peter 2:17, Romans 13:7

Be righteous: Morally right or justifiable; virtuous.
- Don't be wicked: Evil or morally wrong.
- Ephesians 4:24, Ephesians 6:14, 1 Peter 3:11, 1 Peter 2:24

Be self-controlled: Remain calm and reasonable despite provocation.
- Don't be easily provoked: Having feelings that are easily excited and openly displayed.
- Titus 2:2-6, Proverbs 16:32, Proverbs 25:28, 1 Corinthians 7:5, Galatians 5:23

Be selfless: Concerned more with the needs and wishes of others than with one's own; unselfish.
- Don't be selfish: Lacking consideration for others; concerned chiefly with one's own personal profit or pleasure.
- Philippians 2:3

Be sincere: Free from pretense or deceit; proceeding from genuine feelings.
- Don't be insincere: Not expressing genuine feelings.
- Romans 12:9

Be sympathetic: Feeling, showing, or expressing sympathy.
- Don't be unsympathetic: Not feeling, showing, or expressing sympathy.
- 1 Peter 3:8, Romans 12:15, 1 John 3:17. Ephesians 4:32

Be tolerant: Showing willingness to allow the existence of opinions or behavior that one does not necessarily agree with.
- Don't be intolerant: Not tolerant of views, beliefs, or behavior that differ from one's own.
- Romans 12:18

Be trustworthy: Able to be relied on as honest or truthful.
- Don't be unreliable: Not able to be relied upon.
- John 8:26

Be wise: Having or showing experience, knowledge, and good judgement.
- Don't be foolish: Lacking good sense or judgement; unwise.
- Colossians 4:5-6

Annexure E: Answers to wisdom seek-and-find in Chapter 5

The items to be underlined or circled are bolded below:

Gossip, **trustworthiness, kindness,** cruelty, perverse hearts, **blameless ways, generosity, the fruit of our lips,** lying tongue, speaking rashly, **happy hearts,** bribes, **life-giving correction, committing what we do to the Lord,** pride, desire without knowledge, laziness, **kindness to the poor,** being hot-tempered, strife, curses one's father or mother, **humility,** borrowing, injustice, oppressing or exploiting the poor, **being skilled,** gluttony, **prudence, being blameless,** concealing of sins, **working,** stinginess, **defending the rights of the poor and needy.**

Annexure F: References

Chapter 1 - It's all about God

[1] Revelation 1:8, Hebrews 13:8, Psalm 90:2
[2] Romans 9:20, Mark 10:27, Psalm 100:2-3
[3] Isaiah 43:7, Ephesians 1:11-12, Romans 11:33-12:2, 1 Corinthians 10:31
[4] Revelation 3:8, Revelation 3:20, Matthew 7:13-14
[5] Psalm 23:6
[6] John 3:16
[7] Romans 14:17
[8] Romans 10:9
[9] Ephesians 5:7-9
[10] Mark 12:30-31

Chapter 2 - The Tweet

[1] Proverbs 7:2-3

Chapter 3 - Love God

[1] Job 41:11
[2] Romans 10:9-10
[3] Jeremiah 31:33
[4] Mark 12:30
[5] Matthew 10:37
[6] Exodus 20:3
[7] 2 John 1:6, John 14:15
[8] Ephesians 1:4, 1 John 2:6
[9] Ephesians 5:1
[10] 1 John 4:8
[11] Exodus 20:5
[12] Matthew 5: 17-19
[13] Acts 2:38, Acts 17:30
[14] 1 Peter 2:21

Other sources used in writing chapter 3 include:

Looking for God (2022). Available at: https://www.lookingforgod.com/questions-and-answers/category/22/question/1193/ (Accessed: 14 May 2022).

10 REASONS WHY I LOVE THE LORD (2022). Available at: https://www.revival.com/a/469-10-reasons-why-i-love-the-lord (Accessed: 14 May 2022).

Why We Love God (2022). Available at: https://www.desiringgod.org/articles/why-we-love-god (Accessed: 14 May 2022).

Lord, 6. (2022) MY SPIRITUAL BIRTHDAY, Joyful Abundant Life. Available at: https://www.joyfulabundantlife.com/50-reasons-why-i-love-the-lord/ (Accessed: 14 May 2022).

Love God Is To Obey Him.

- If you love me, obey my commandments. (John 14:15, NLT)
- That's the whole story. Here now is my final conclusion: Fear God and obey his commands, for this is everyone's duty. (Ecclesiastes 12:13, NLT)
- Loving God means keeping his commandments, and his commandments are not burdensome. (1 John 5:3, NLT)
- When you obey my commandments, you remain in my love, just as I obey my Father's commandments and remain in his love. (John 15:10, NLT)

Abrugar, V. (2018) How to Love God According to the Bible, Inspiring Tips. Available at: https://inspiringtips.com/how-to-love-god-according-to-the-bible/ (Accessed: 14 May 2022).

Chapter 4 - Love Others
[1] Romans 12:1-2
[2] Romans 10:9-10
[3] 1 Timothy 1:18-19
[4] Matthew 7:7-8

Chapter 5 - Living a Life of Love
[1] Matthew 7:11
[2] Matthew 7:7

Chapter 6 - Transformation and Renewal
[1] 1 Corinthians 10:31
[2] 2 Corinthians 13:5
[3] Matthew 7:7
[4] Titus 3:4-7

Chapter 7 - Love and Love
[1] Hebrews 12:1-2
[2] 1 John 4:9
[3] 1 Peter 1: 16-17
[4] Philippians 1:9-10

Annexure A

God is…

1.   Mercy (2018). Available at: https://www.encyclopedia.com/philosophy-and-religion/bible/bible-general/mercy (Accessed: 8 June 2022).

Other sources used in this section:

- **Acquaint thyself with God.** Tozer, AW. The Knowledge of the Holy (AW Tozer Series) (p. 66). GENERAL PRESS. Kindle Edition.
- **The Joy of Knowing God** (https://bible.org/series/joy-knowing-god) Richard L. Strauss

Annexure D

1. Oxford Languages and Google - English | Oxford Languages (2022). Available at: https://languages.oup.com/google-dictionary-en/ (Accessed: 9 June 2022).